PETER

written by

Melissa C. Downey

Susan L. Lingo

illustrated by

Roy Green

STANDARD
PUBLISHING
Cincinnati, Ohio

Library of Congress Number 92-61783

ISBN 0-7847-0034-6

The Standard Publishing Company, Cincinnati, Ohio.
A Division of Standex International Corporation.

00 99 98 97 96 95 94 93   5 4 3 2 1

Peter

John 1:35-42; Matthew 4:18-20; Luke 5:4-9; Matthew 14:29, 30; 16:16-18;
John 13:36-38; 21:1-20; Acts 1:6-11; 2:1-42; 10:9-35; 12:1-17

"Simon! S-i-m-o-n!" Andrew came running, shouting between breaths. "You've got to come with me! I've met the Messiah, the Christ!"

Simon looked up. He and his brother Andrew were from Bethsaida, which means "house of fish." They, like many others in that town, were fishermen. But business had been a little slow lately because Andrew had been spending a lot of time listening to the strange prophet on the Jordan River, John the Baptist, while Peter tended to business.

"What did you say, Andrew?"

"I've met the Christ! Come quickly and meet Him."

"You don't mean John, do you?" Simon asked.

"No!" Andrew replied. "The one John said was coming after him. His name is Jesus. He came to the river today, and John said, 'Look, the Lamb of God!' I not only looked—I followed Him. This is He, Simon. This is the One!"

Simon got up to go and meet Jesus. When they came to Jesus, He said to Simon, "You are Simon, son of John. . . ." Simon wanted to say, "How did you know that?" But Jesus was not finished speaking. "You will be called Peter," He said.

"Peter, the rock," Simon thought. "Now what kind of name is that?" he wondered. He decided he would follow this Jesus and find out. He, his brother, and a few others traveled with Jesus for some time. Jesus did remarkable things and taught powerful lessons about serving God. Then they returned home.

One day, as Simon Peter and Andrew were casting their nets from the shore, they saw Jesus coming to meet them.

"Come follow me," He said, "and I will make you fishers of men." They dropped their nets and followed Jesus. The brothers became two of Jesus' first disciples.

As a disciple of Jesus, Simon Peter had many adventures. One day after teaching the people, Jesus told the brothers to cast their nets from the boat. Fishing during the day was usually not successful; but they caught more fish than they had caught fishing all night! Imagine Jesus the carpenter teaching fishermen to fish! Peter was beginning to understand that Jesus was no ordinary man. On another occasion, Peter actually walked on the water with Jesus! Peter soon learned, as

Jesus' disciple, that every day was a new adventure!

He watched as Jesus lovingly healed and cared for the people. He listened as Jesus taught about the heavenly Father's love. One day, Simon Peter said to Jesus, "You are the Son of God!" Jesus said, "Your name is Peter (small rock). On *this* rock (solid rock) I will build my church."

Peter loved Jesus. At the last supper, Peter told Jesus that he loved Him enough to die for Him. But Jesus answered, "Will you really die for me? Before the rooster crows, you will say three times that you don't know me." After the soldiers had taken Jesus away, three times Peter was asked if he knew Jesus. Each time he said "no." Then the rooster crowed. Peter remembered what Jesus had said. Peter was angry with himself and very sad.

After Jesus arose from the dead, He came to the disciples by the Sea of Galilee. Jesus asked, "Simon, son of John, do you love me?" Peter answered, "Yes!" Jesus asked him the same question three times, one for each time Peter had denied Him. Each time Peter answered, "Yes!" Peter's heart was glad because Jesus had forgiven him.

After this, Jesus told the disciples to wait in Jerusalem until His gift of the Holy Spirit came to the disciples. Ten days after Jesus returned to Heaven, the disciples were together in Jerusalem. Suddenly a noise like a strong wind filled the house. Flames like tongues of fire came on each of them. They began to speak in different languages. They left the house and went into the city. With the power of the Holy Spirit, Peter and the others spoke to the crowd of people from many countries and told them about Jesus. Three thousand people believed in Jesus and were baptized that day. Peter continued to serve Jesus by preaching and healing the sick.

One day Peter saw a vision of Heaven opening up. He saw what looked like a big sheet being lowered to the earth by its four corners. In it were animals of all kinds. Then he heard a voice say, "Get up Peter, kill and eat." But Peter refused. He thought that some of the animals were "unclean," which meant not good to eat. But the Lord told him that whatever He made was clean and good. After the vision, some men came to Peter's door. They told him of Cornelius, a Roman soldier who wanted to know about Jesus. Immediately, Peter understood what the vision meant. Some would have said a Roman soldier was "unclean," that Peter should not go to his house to tell him about Jesus. But Peter knew that God wanted him to teach *all* people about Jesus.

Peter continued to teach about Jesus. Soon King Herod heard about Peter and put Peter in jail. But while Peter was in jail, the church prayed for him. An angel came to Peter in the night and said, "Peter! Hurry!" The chains fell off Peter's hands. Peter followed the angel out. They went past the first and second guards, but no one saw them! When they came to the street, the angel left him. Peter went straight to the house where the church was meeting. How they rejoiced to see him and were amazed when he told them what had happened!

Peter

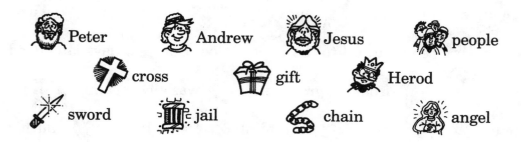

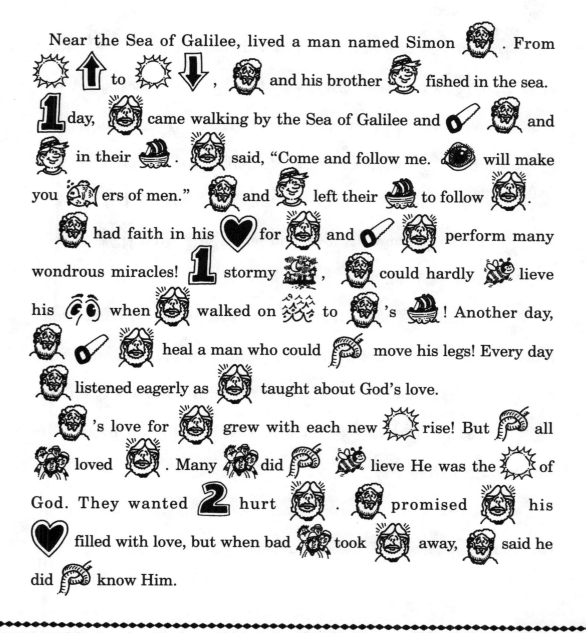

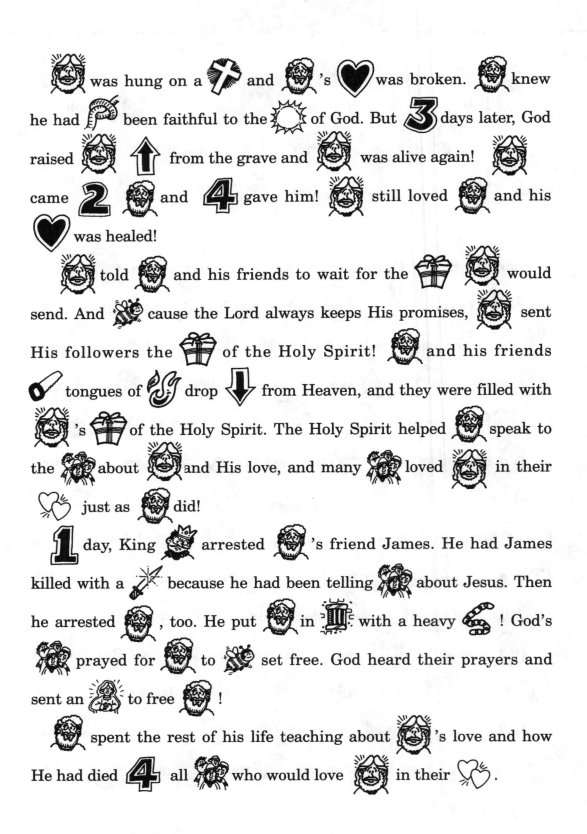

was hung on a and 's was broken. knew he had been faithful to the of God. But **3** days later, God raised from the grave and was alive again! came **2** and **4** gave him! still loved and his was healed!

told and his friends to wait for the would send. And cause the Lord always keeps His promises, sent His followers the of the Holy Spirit! and his friends tongues of drop from Heaven, and they were filled with 's of the Holy Spirit. The Holy Spirit helped speak to the about and His love, and many loved in their just as did!

day, King arrested 's friend James. He had James killed with a because he had been telling about Jesus. Then he arrested , too. He put in with a heavy ! God's prayed for to set free. God heard their prayers and sent an to free !

spent the rest of his life teaching about 's love and how He had died **4** all who would love in their .

Mark 1:16-18

"When Jesus was walking by Lake Galilee, he saw Simon and Simon's brother, Andrew. They were fishermen and were throwing a net into the lake to catch fish. Jesus said to them, 'Come and follow me. I will make you fishermen for men.' So Simon and Andrew immediately left their nets and followed him" Mark 1:16-18 (ICB).

Make Your Own Rebus

Cut out the pictures below. Then paste or tape them into place to fill in the missing words of this Scripture.

When ☐ was walking by ☐ Galilee, he ☐ ☐ and Simon's brother, ☐. They were ☐ and were throwing a ☐ into the ☐ to catch ☐. ☐ said to them, "Come and follow me. I will make you ☐ for ☐." So ☐ and ☐ immediately left their ☐s and followed him.

Jesus	Lake	saw	Simon	Andrew
fishermen	net	lake	fish	Jesus
fishermen	men	Simon	Andrew	net

Fishing Gear

What were the two tools Peter used most as a fisherman?

Follow the directions below to find out.
(The teacher may wish to read the directions aloud.)

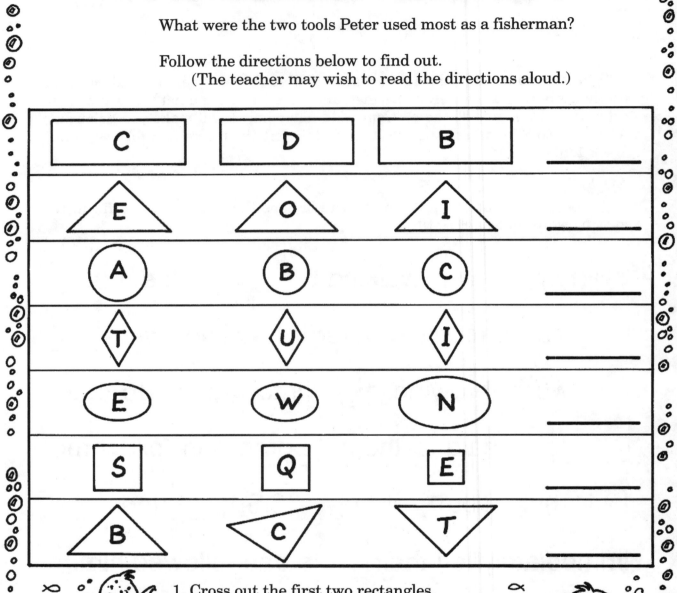

C	D	B	_____
E	O	I	_____
A	B	C	_____
T	U	I	_____
E	W	N	_____
S	Q	E	_____
B	C	T	_____

1. Cross out the first two rectangles.
2. Color in the first and last triangles.
3. Draw a line through the small circles.
4. Color in the second and the third diamonds.
5. Cross out the small ovals.
6. Draw a line through the large squares.
7. Color in the first and second triangles.
8. Write the remaining letters in the blanks.

___ ___ ___ and ___ ___ ___

Peter and Andrew spent many hours fishing on the Sea of Galilee. Do you suppose they ever told each other "fishy" jokes? Untangle the fishing lines below to find the answers to these fishy riddles!

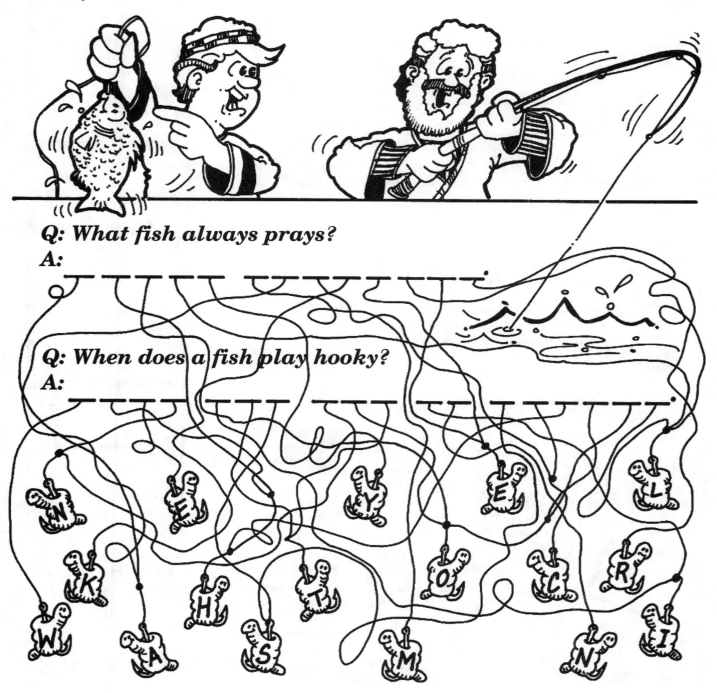

Q: What fish always prays?
A:

Q: When does a fish play hooky?
A:

Antonyms ⇒ Opposite

Antonyms are words that mean the opposite of each other. For example, *happy* and *sad* are antonyms. They mean the opposite of each other.

What are the antonyms for these words:

good   _____

hard   _____

long   _____

empty   _____

day   _____

Answer Box
full
night
short
bad
soft

To describe Peter, find the antonyms for these words.

weak   _____

shy   _____

cowardly   _____

foolish   _____

mean   _____

selfish   _____

little   _____

Answer Box
big
strong
kind
outgoing
giving
wise
brave

Did You Know?

What did Peter look like?
The earliest pictures of Peter show him having dark curly hair and a curly beard. He had tanned skin from being outside so much. He was strong because he had to lift heavy nets into his boat.

The Best Gift

Do you have a brother or sister? Do you ever give gifts to him/her? What would be the best gift you could give?

Peter had a little brother named Andrew. Andrew gave the best gift ever to his older brother Peter. To find out what this gift was, color in all the G's, B's, L's and Y's in the puzzle. Then write the remaining letters in the blanks below.

A	B	N	G	D	G	R	L	E	Y	W
L	G	B	Y	B	G	Y	L	Y	B	L
G	T	Y	O	B	O	G	K	Y	L	B
B	L	G	Y	L	G	B	L	G	Y	L
P	G	E	B	T	L	Y	E	G	R	G
Y	B	G	Y	L	Y	G	B	Y	G	B
G	Y	L	L	T	Y	B	O	G	L	G
B	G	Y	L	G	Y	B	L	G	Y	B
L	B	M	G	E	Y	E	L	T	G	Y
B	G	Y	L	B	G	Y	L	B	G	Y
L	J	B	E	G	S	L	U	G	S	B

__ __ __ __ __ __   __ __ __ __   __ __ __

__ __   __ __ __ __   __ __ __ __ __

Have you met Jesus? Have you shared this gift with your brother or sister? Jesus is the greatest gift of all, the best gift you can give to everyone.

Walking on Water

Story Diorama

Figure A:
Front (Box Lid)

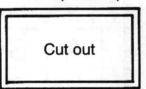

Cut out

Needed
- 1 shoe box with lid
- 3 1/4" dowels cut 3" longer than box
- 2 1/4" dowels 5" long (soda straws may be used)
- construction paper
- glue, tape, scissors, and crayons

Figure B:
Side

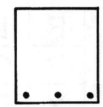

Punch holes in box sides.

Directions
Prepare Box (should be done by an adult or older child)
1. Cut out lid as indicated in Figure A.
2. Punch holes in box as indicated in Figure B.
3. Cut curved slits in box as indicated in Figure C.
4. Make copies of Peter and Jesus (from next page).

Figure C:
Top

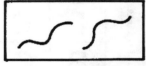

cut 1/4" slits

Prepare Objects (may be done by younger children)
1. Make two waves of light and dark blue construction paper, using pattern on next page. Glue or tape to dowel, leaving 1 1/2" margin on each side.
2. Make boat with sail of brown and white construction paper, using pattern on next page; glue or tape to dowel 1 1/2" from right end of dowel.
3. Cut out and color Jesus and Peter; glue or tape each to the appropriate dowel/straw.

Assemble Diorama
1. Place the boat dowel in diorama first at the back of the diorama.
2. Insert dowel/straw with Peter through the top.
3. Place the light blue wave (middle) and then the dark blue wave (front).
4. Place the dowel/straw with Jesus through the top.
5. Secure lid to box with glue or tape

Figure D:
Completed Diorama

Use the diorama to tell the story of Jesus and Peter walking on the water. As the story is told, the children can move the water and figures.

Jesus

Peter

To make it easier for the children, direct them to cut out figures and boat on the dark outlines.

Fold

Glue/tape to dowel

Fold

Fold

Glue/tape to dowel

Fold

Peter has been out fishing and needs to figure out how many pounds of fish he has caught. Can you help Peter?

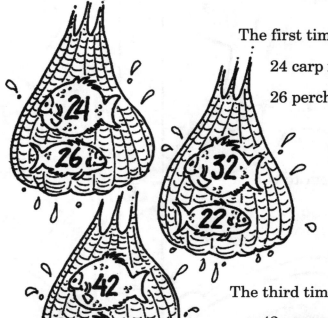

The first time he pulled in his net, he caught

24 carp x 2 pounds each = _____

26 perch x 1 pound each = _____

The second time he pulled in his net, he caught

32 carp x 2 pounds each = _____

22 perch x 1 pound each = _____

The third time he pulled in his net, he caught

42 carp x 2 pounds each = _____

56 perch x 1 pound each = _____

If Peter sells the fish for $1.00 a pound, how much money will he make?

pounds of carp ____ + ____ + ____ = ____

pounds of perch ____ + ____ + ____ = ____

____ + ____ = ____ pounds of fish

____ x $1.00 = $ _____

Answer Box		
56	84	48
26	64	22
196	104	300

Free Key!

Chains! Chains! You're locked up in chains, and there's only one who holds the key. Solve the puzzle below to find the one who will set you free!

Directions

Find the five identical keys and circle them. Then unscramble the letters in the matching keys on the spaces below to find the key who sets you free!

____ ____ ____ ____ ____ is the Key who will set me free!

Home on

Jesus called Peter a "rock," but Jesus himself was *The* Rock on which He built His church! Climb your way "Home" to the church that sits on the Rock!

Welcome

Slide down

Rock 'n Roll

Rock 'n Roll

Rock 'n Roll

Step up!

Rock 'n Roll

Start

Rock 'n Roll

the Rock

Rock 'n Roll

You Need
1 die
2-4 players
paper fastener (to attach cardboard arrow to spinner)

Directions
1. Take turns spinning for move.
2. If you land on "Rock 'n Roll," use the die to roll your next move!
3. First player to the HOME ON THE ROCK is the winner!

1 2 1 2 3 Lose 1 Turn

Scripture Memory

Matthew 16:19

Peter spent his life learning that Jesus was the key to set him free, and no chains on earth are too strong for Jesus! Make the Heavenly Key Chain below to help you remember, as Peter did, that with Jesus in your heart you truly have the key to Heaven!

You Need
poster board
paper punch
key chain (or yarn)

Directions
1. Color the keys below. Glue page to poster board.
2. Cut out the keys and punch a hole at the top of each one. (Younger children can cut along the rectangular lines. Older children may choose to cut out the key shapes.)
3. String verse, in order, on key chain or yarn.

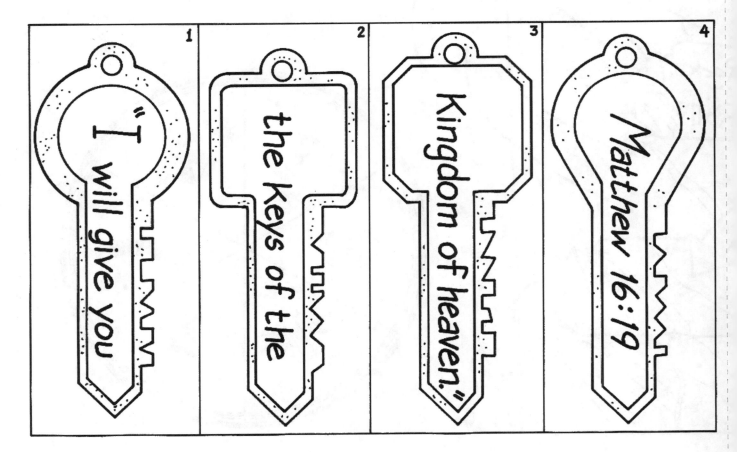

1. "I will give you
2. the keys of the
3. Kingdom of heaven."
4. Matthew 16:19

Locked in Love

Peter told Jesus he would go to jail with Jesus, he would die for Jesus, and he would love Jesus forever! But when Jesus was arrested, Peter did not keep his first two promises. He denied he even knew Him! But Peter never stopped loving Jesus, and Jesus never stopped loving Peter! Love for Jesus was the special key Peter kept in his heart so that at last, Peter did keep his promises —he went to jail and died for Him! Jesus was the key to Peter's heart!

Make this "Locked in Love" heart and key to remind you Jesus is the key to your heart, too!

Directions

1. Color the heart and key or use them as patterns to make them from construction paper.
2. Cut out the heart and key carefully.
3. Snip one end of the lock and slip on the key. Then tape the lock back together.

The Broken Promise

I made Jesus a promise
   that I didn't keep—
Now all I can do while my heart breaks
   is weep.

"I'll love you forever!"
   in faith I implored Him.
Then I pushed Him aside, turned my back
   and ignored Him.

How will I stand this
   unbearable pain?
I'm a promise that's broken and
   hung out in shame!

How could He ever
   call me His friend?
How can He ever
   love me again?

Please see my heart, Lord!
   I know you're the Son—
And I'm asking forgiveness
   for what I have done!

The Lord Jesus gives mercy and
   love till the end;
He is risen this day and . . .
   HE LOVES ME AGAIN!

The ♡ Inside Me

You Need
felt (4 colors)
markers

Directions
1. Cut out the pieces below.
2. Use these pieces as patterns and cut new pieces from felt.
3. Draw details on the felt pieces as needed.
4. Place the pieces on as you recite the poem below.
(Note: The felt pieces will stick to most sweaters, sweatshirts, flannel shirts and fuzzy tops. Use also on flannel boards—or on desk tops.)

This is the HEART inside me.

This is the CHAIN that carries the pain that binds the heart inside me.

This is the LOCK that tightens the chain that carries the pain that binds the heart inside me.

This is the KEY that sets me free and opens the lock that loosens the chain that carried the pain and frees the heart inside me!

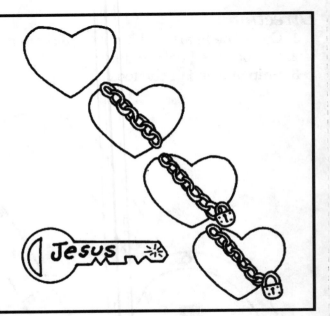

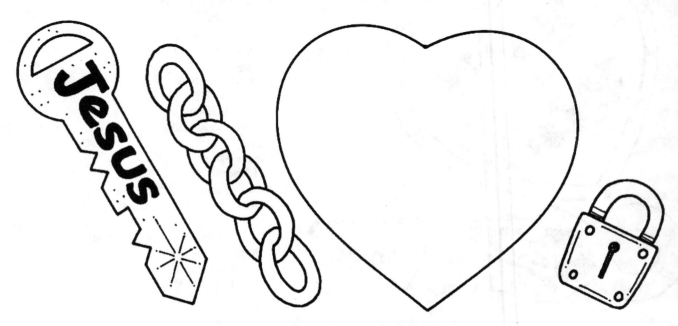

Act It Out

The Last Great Catch

Characters: Peter, Andrew, James, John, Philip, Thomas, Nathanael, Jesus, and Narrator (may be the teacher)

Narrator: A few days ago, Jesus arose from the dead! Peter and John had found the tomb empty. Later they saw Jesus. Now, seven of the disciples are at Peter's house. So much has happened over the last few weeks! The disciples are not sure what to do next.

Scene One:
Peter's house, men sitting around table. It is early evening.

Peter: I'm really not sure what we should do next. But wouldn't it be good to be out in the boat?
Andrew: We haven't been out on the water in days.
James: Isn't your boat just down the shore, Peter?
Peter: Yes. Yes! Let's go fishing!
John: I'll get the nets!
Philip: I'll get the oars!
Nathanael: Let's go!

Scene Two
The men are in the boat with a net cast on the left side. (A simple boat can be an arrangement of six chairs in groups of two. A small sheet can serve as a net.)

Narrator: It is almost morning. The men have been fishing all night and are tired. Their net is empty.
Andrew: (tired) The sun will be up soon.
Nathanael: Thomas, help me check the net again. Maybe there will be fish in it this time.
Thomas: I doubt it.
(They pull in an empty net from the left side of boat.)
Peter: That does it! Time to go in! We've finished all night and haven't caught a thing . . . I bet if Jesus were here, He'd tell us where the fish were!
(Men begin to row boat to shore.)
James: I'm almost too tired to row.
John: We're almost home! I can barely see the shore—someone has a fire going.
Jesus: (shouting from shore) Friends! Have you caught anything?
Fishermen: (loudly) No, not a fish!
Jesus: Throw your net to the right side of the boat—you'll find some fish there!
Peter: What do you think, men? Let's try one more time.
(They throw the net to the right side.)
Nathanael: Wow! Listen to those fish flop!

Thomas: Net's almost full!

Peter: Let's pull it in, guys.

Thomas, Philip, James: We can't lift the net! It will tear!

Peter: Then we'll just drag it along.

John: Wait! That's Jesus on the shore!

Peter: What? Jesus? YES it is!

(Peter jumps out of the boat and heads to the shore. The rest follow in the boat, dragging the net.)

Scene Three
On the shore; fire, bread, fish (A pretend fire
can be made with a small circle of stones and a few sticks.)

Narrator: Jesus is standing by the fire. He has prepared bread and fish for the men's breakfast. Peter is very happy to be with Jesus again. The men bring the boat to shore. Jesus greets the men and they walk to the fire.

Jesus: Bring some more fish! I've already cooked some and have some bread ready. Come friends and eat!

Peter: (speaking to Andrew) Didn't I tell you that if Jesus were here, He'd tell us where the fish are!

Net o' Fish: A Counting Activity

Needed
Fish crackers
Napkins (nets)
Pencils and paper

Directions
Divide the children into groups of 3 or 4 and assign one child to be the record keeper.

Give each child in each group a net o' fish (crackers in napkin).

Each net should have a different number of fish. (The number of fish given should vary with skill level.)

Have each child count the number of fish in his net.

The record keeper writes down the number of fish of each group member; then the group adds the numbers to get a group total. To check the total, the children can trade nets and repeat the process.

When you are finished, allow the children to eat the fish!

♪ Scripture Song ♪♪

"Come, let us sing for joy to the Lord."

Psalm 95:1

This song is based on John 21:15-17, where Jesus asked Peter to love and tend His followers, His sheep! Use the actions on the right side of the page to act out the song as you sing the words! (Sing to the tune of "Mary Had a Little Lamb.")

Tend My Sheep

If you love Me, tend My sheep,
tend My sheep,
tend My sheep;
If you love Me, tend My sheep and
teach them of my love.

patting motion

If you love Me, feed My sheep,
feed My sheep,
feed My sheep;
If you love Me, feed My sheep and
teach them of My love.

feeding motion

If you love Me, hold My sheep,
hold My sheep,
hold My sheep;
If you love Me, hold My sheep and
teach them of My love.

cradling motion

"Sing to him a new song."

Psalm 33:3

Firey Words of Faith

When did Peter speak with fiery words of faith?

Fill in the missing letters to solve the puzzle below. They will reveal the day Peter first spoke with "fiery faith."

Em ⬡ owered by God's

On ⬡ and

O ⬡ ly, came a

fiery ⬡ estimony.

And so th ⬡

"Ro ⬡ k" of Jesus had sung

when G ⬡ d set

flame ⬡ to

Peter's ⬡ ongue!

Now rearrange the letters in the bold circles to find the One Peter spoke of!

God's ___ ___ ___!

Picture Spelling

The first letters of the pictures will spell out the names of animals that might have been in the sheet of Peter's vision.

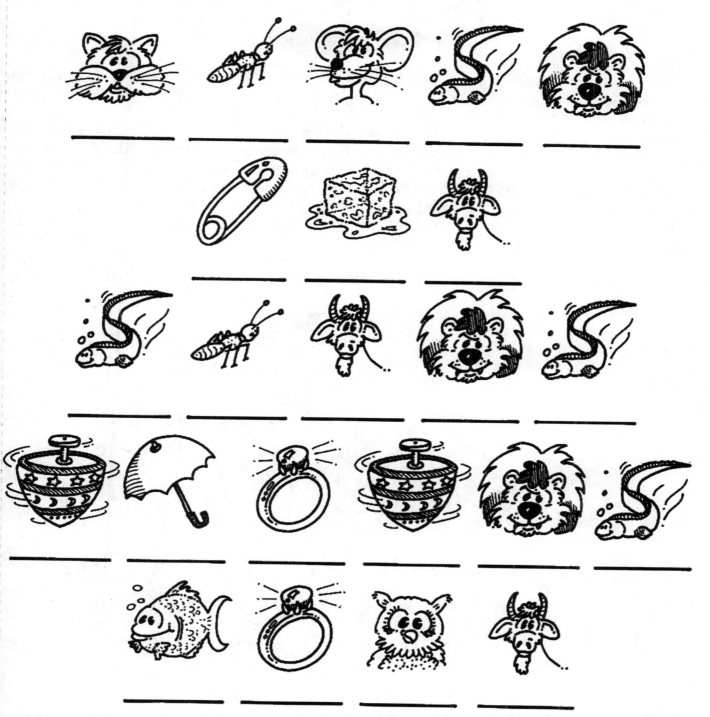

A *captive* is someone bound or tied, not free. Peter was held captive by King Herod, who did not love the Lord. Sent to prison for teaching people about Jesus and how He died for their sins, Peter was chained to a wall and held captive.

But these iron chains were not the only chains that bound Peter! Strong chains of love and faith bound Peter to Jesus! Each link in this heavenly chain was forged with faith—strong and sure, an everlasting chain from Jesus' heart to Peter's heart! And because Peter was bound to Jesus, he was truly set free! Free to love, to forgive and to live forever as a child of God. No earthly chains were as strong as the heavenly link that bound Peter to Jesus!

Peter was a captive, in chains, and set free by the Lord's angel. But most glorious of all, Peter was truly captive-ated and set free by Jesus!

"God has made Jesus both Lord and Christ"—Acts 2:36 (ICB).

Find the above Scripture verse and color in the links as you work your way through this a-maze-ing chain of glory and love from God!

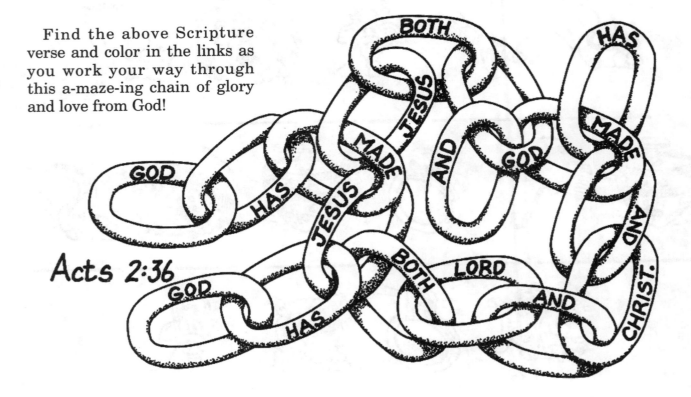

Acts 2:36

Key Verses!

Use each "key" to find a key Scripture verse that tells how we, as Peter, have been set free!
(All verses are from the *International Children's Bible*.)

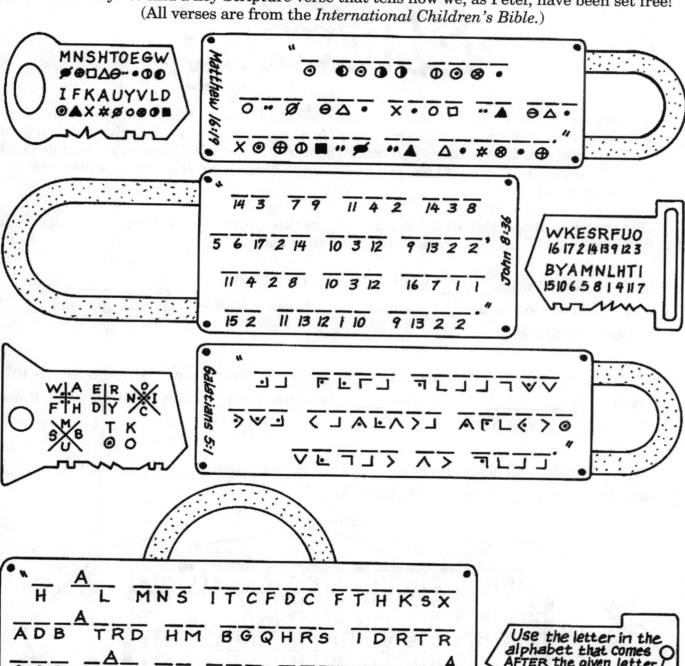

Jesus came to us as a "living stone," strong and sure for us to build our everlasting lives upon! To believers, Jesus is a firm foundation of love and faith. But for those who do not love the Lord, He becomes the rock that will cause them to slip and fall! Keep your love, faith and obedience in Jesus, the living stone, and your feet will stand on solid rock—otherwise . . . your slip may show!

Using your ICB Bible, 1 Peter 2:4-8, fill in the missing words below. Then find each one in the Word Hunt! (You will hunt some words more than once!)

The Lord Jesus is the _____ that lives (v. 4). He was the _____ God _____. Come to _____ (v. 4). You also are like _____ stones. Let yourselves be used to build a spiritual _____ (v. 5). The Scripture says:

"I will put a _____ in the ground in _____ (v. 6). Everything will be built on this important and _____ _____ (v. 6). This _____ is worth much to you who believe (v. 7). It has become the _____ (v. 7)."

To those who do not believe, he is a _____ that causes people to _____ (v. 8). They _____ because they do not _____ what God says (v. 8).

A	R	P	C	O	R	N	E	R	S	T	O	N	E	L	C	E
J	E	R	U	S	A	L	E	M	R	O	K	C	T	O	S	O
S	N	E	O	T	L	I	N	R	S	T	O	N	E	K	T	N
R	O	C	K	O	E	V	C	O	T	E	M	P	L	E	O	E
T	E	I	C	N	M	I	K	N	U	M	L	H	I	N	N	T
C	H	O	S	E	P	N	H	I	M	L	T	S	N	O	E	S
R	C	U	O	N	L	G	R	O	B	S	T	U	M	B	L	E
O	K	S	T	O	N	E	C	K	L	R	O	K	T	E	N	N
C	E	R	N	A	S	T	O	N	E	C	H	O	S	Y	E	T

Which Came First??

Our Bible is divided into two parts:

Part 1	**Part 2**
Old Testament	New Testament
This is about God's love for Israel and the coming of Jesus.	This is about Jesus and His Church.
It was written before Jesus was born.	It was written after Jesus was born.

Where do we find the stories about Peter? _____

Which Came First?

First, put a number (1-10) in front of each of the following events to indicate in what order they happened. Which events are from the Old Testament and which are from the New Testament? Match the event with its place on the time line to find out.

___ Noah built the ark

___ God created the world

___ David fought Goliath

___ Daniel and the lion's den

___ Moses, 10 Commandments

___ Jesus was born

___ The church began at Pentecost

___ Peter became Jesus' disciple

___ Jesus arose

___ Jesus died on the cross

OLD TESTAMENT | NEW TESTAMENT

1 2 3 4 5 6 7 8 9 10

Riddling Review

I am the wave-walker
and the fish-provider
I am the healer
I am God's only Son
I am the Holy One

I have wings and a comb
I'm a farmer's alarm
Peter remembers me
for my crows time 3

I am a net-caster
and a hearing rock
I am a fisher of men

I am Jesus' gift
to believers in Him
I came as tongues of fire
and the sound of a mighty wind

I'm thrown into the sea
I am a fish catcher
and a fisherman's friend

I am the younger brother
I am a fishing partner
I took Peter to Jesus

Answers: Jesus, Peter, Net, Rooster, Holy Spirit, Andrew

Rock 'n Roll!

Did you know that with your name on Heaven's Roll and your feet on the Rock of Jesus, you're a member of the best "rock 'n roll" group around? And that should be music to your soul!

If you ask me what's my cup of tea;
my favorite cereal bowl . . .
it's such a simple choice for me:
I love that "Rock 'n Roll"!

It's not the songs that you may
know on every blaring stereo,
but it's real music to my soul:
I love each beat of "Rock 'n Roll"

Fill in the missing vowels to complete these two Scripture verses!

"H__ st__ __d m__ __n __ r__ck" (Psalm 40:2, ICB).

"Y__ __ sh __ __ld b__ h__ppy b__c__ __s__ y__ __r

n__m__s __r__ wr__tt__n __n h__ __v__n"

(Luke 10:20, ICB).

M·A·P·P·I·N·G Major Moments

Match the number of each event with its place on the map.
Then fill in or circle the correct answer.

1. Jesus calls Peter to follow Him. This is near the Sea of _____ .

2. Peter walks on the water with Jesus in the Sea of _____ .

3. Peter says that he doesn't know Jesus. This happens in the city of _____ .

5. During Pentecost, the Holy Spirit comes to the disciples. Peter preaches to the crowd about Jesus. Jerusalem is (north or south) of Capernaum.

4. After Jesus' resurrection the disciples go fishing. Jesus tells them where to fish. Jesus asks Peter if he loves Him. This happens near the village of _____ .

6. Peter sees the vision of the sheet filled with animals. This happens in the city of _____ .

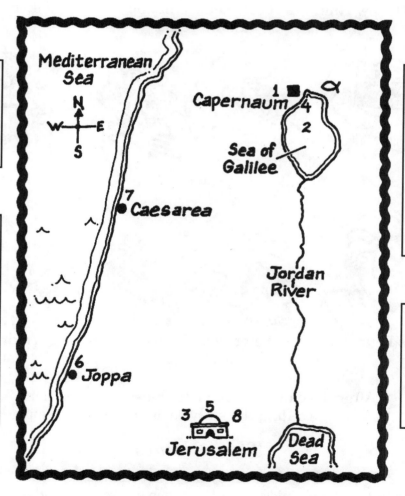

7. Cornelius lived here. He wanted Peter to teach him about Jesus. Cornelius lived in the city of _____ .

8. Peter is freed from prison by an angel. Jerusalem is (east or west) of the Dead Sea.

Picturing Peter

The pictures below are of major events in Peter's life. One picture is out of order in each row. Which picture is it? Circle it and then draw an arrow to where the picture should go.

Jesus calls Peter to follow Him.

Peter denies that he knows Jesus.

Peter walks on water.

Vision of the Sheet

Pentecost

Rescue from Jail

Jesus forgives Peter.

Peter tells Cornelius about Jesus.

Andrew tells Peter about Jesus.

After the children complete the activity, let them take turns telling the story each picture represents.

Three Names

Peter was known by three names.
Place the first letter of each picture in the space above it to find each of his names!